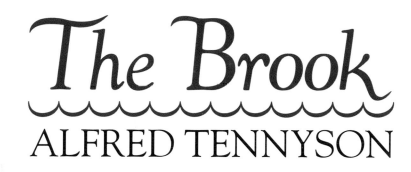

# The Brook

## ALFRED TENNYSON

*illustrations by Charles Micucci*

ORCHARD BOOKS
*New York*

Illustrations copyright © 1994 by Charles Micucci
All rights reserved. No part of this book may be reproduced or
transmitted in any form or by any means, electronic or mechanical,
including photocopying, recording, or by any information storage or
retrieval system, without permission in writing from the Publisher.

Orchard Books
95 Madison Avenue, New York, NY 10016

Manufactured in the United States of America
Printed by Barton Press, Inc.      Bound by Horowitz/Rae
The text of this book is set in 18 point Goudy Old Style.
The illustrations are watercolor and pencil reproduced in full color.
Book design by Charles Micucci

10   9   8   7   6   5   4   3   2   1

Library of Congress Cataloging-in-Publication Data
Tennyson, Alfred Tennyson, Baron, 1809–1892.
   The brook / Alfred Tennyson ; illustrations by Charles Micucci.
      p.      cm.
   Summary: An illustrated presentation of the poem by a well-known
nineteenth-century British poet, inspired by a brook that flowed near his house.
      ISBN 0-531-06854-4. — ISBN 0-531-08704-2 (lib. bdg.)
      1. Rivers—Juvenile poetry.   2. Children's poetry, English.
   [1. Rivers—Poetry.   2. English poetry.]      I. Micucci, Charles, ill.      II. Title.
   PR5555.B6      1994      821′.8—dc20      93-46404

"The Brook," which is read by children all over the world,
     is actually a group of verses from a much larger poem, also called "The Brook."
          It was originally published in 1855 in a collection called Maud, and Other Poems.

For men may come and men may go,
But I go on forever.

I come from haunts of coot and hern,
I make a sudden sally,
And sparkle out among the fern,
To bicker down a valley.

By thirty hills I hurry down,
  Or slip between the ridges,
By twenty thorps, a little town,
  And half a hundred bridges.

Till last by Philip's farm I flow
To join the brimming river,
For men may come and men may go,
But I go on forever.

I chatter over stony ways,
In little sharps and trebles,
I bubble into eddying bays,
I babble on the pebbles.

With many a curve my banks I fret
By many a field and fallow,
And many a fairy foreland set
With willow-weed and mallow.

I chatter, chatter, as I flow
To join the brimming river,
For men may come and men may go,
But I go on forever.

I wind about and in and out,
With here a blossom sailing,
And here and there a lusty trout,
And here and there a grayling,

And here and there a foamy flake
Upon me, as I travel
With many a silvery water-break
Above the golden gravel,

And draw them all along, and flow
To join the brimming river,
For men may come and men may go,
But I go on forever.

I steal by lawns and grassy plots,
I slide by hazel covers;
I move the sweet forget-me-nots
That grow for happy lovers.

I slip, I slide, I gloom, I glance,
Among my skimming swallows;
I make the netted sunbeam dance
Against my sandy shallows.

I murmur under moon and stars
In brambly wildernesses;
I linger by my shingly bars,
I loiter round my cresses;

And out again I curve and flow
To join the brimming river,
For men may come and men may go,
But I go on forever.

# Glossary

**coot**.....a plump water bird similar to a duck but with big unwebbed toes

**cresses**.....leafy plants that grow in running water

**grayling**.....a silver fish with a long blue and pink fin

**hern**.....also called a heron, a tall, skinny bird with a long bill and large wings

**mallow**.....large flowers that frequently grow near streams

**sally**.....a sudden rush, like rapids in a stream

**thorp**.....a small village

ALFRED TENNYSON was born in 1809 in Somersby, Lincolnshire, England.
Like many great English poets, Tennyson found inspiration in nature.
Often his words are phrased in rhythms heard in the outdoors,
like the sound of water running over stones or of waves rushing in and out.
"The Brook" was inspired by a stream that flowed near his house.
After a long life of writing many other famous poems like "The Lady of Shalott"
and "The Charge of the Light Brigade," he died in 1892.